When I Stepped Over The Rainbow

Robin Dozier- Ghent

INTRODUTION

My heart's desire is to help encourage others to become proficient at being themselves. I want to see people enjoy life in the manner in which God designed life to be lived.

As an author and speaker, I thought *When I Stepped Over The Rainbow* by Robin Ghent was unique, simple and to the point. I was inspired by its format and am now thinking about writing a similar book for financial advisors who want to help individuals reach personal financial mastery.

When I Stepped Over The Rainbow is not fluff – it is a straight-forward, practical explanation of the rules for becoming Biblically Responsible for changing your life and never again blaming anyone for your personal circumstances.

Every page is crammed full of useful hints and tips that you can profit from.

Joseph Tolbert Jr.

CONTENTS

ACKNOWLEDGMENTS

I thank God for giving me a vision, my loving husband,
my mother and my children and grandchildren. This book
is written in memory of my grandparents John and Edna
Lewis

WHEN I STEPPED OVER THE RAINBOW

This is probably the hardest story I ever had to write. I guess it's because it made me take a good look at myself. The searching for completeness is always difficult. The things we are looking for is always inside of ourselves but we often search for those things in others. We search for Love in others when we must love ourselves first. I have had a great life. My family was there for me. I was the oldest child. My grandparents were a solid foundation for my family. They had their own business.

I remember growing up with love, happiness and peace. Education was always stressed in our home. My mother was a positive factor for the person I am now. She is a strong woman. "Cant" was not an option when it came to determining whether or not a project could be done. Therefore, I was always in a positive place. Peace was always in my home. When my sister and brother came along we loved each other very much.

When I Stepped Over The Rainbow

As I grew up we went to church and we knew about God because my grandparents were Southern Christians. Life for me was great. I was raised in Massachusetts went to the best of schools and my mother made sure that we had activities to do. Watching TV was not one of them. I guess that is why TV is not my favorite, I like to read, and I like to write.

This story is about how I stepped over the rainbow was a revealing chapter in my life. I thought everyone knew these things but now I find out that they did not. I guess I lived a sheltered life and continue to stay in the quiet life style.

The Angels Kissed my Heart

The way to get over the rainbow is to get to a quiet place. This is not always a place in your home or even in your car, it is in your mind. This is a place where all the outside noise no longer can get to the real self. It takes time and it takes practice. If you start-off by getting a favorite chair and every morning you go there for 5 minutes then 10 minutes and the more, you go there you will be able to get to the quiet place.

I started by taking my dining room and setting up an altar. This was my space. I would place pictures of my loved ones there and I would write down the things I desired on a poster board.

Each day I would go to my place. I would not always ask God for things I would sometimes just thank him for the things we had already done.

To my surprise, I checked my list and the things I asked for began to manifest. I began with writing a book. This was when the angels kissed my heart. It was about 3 am in the morning and I was awakened by a thought "Meet Me at the Bus Stop". The Holy Spirit spoke to me and told me to get a pen and paper. I did. I began to write a story, which turned into a book. The idea was to write a self-help book for young women to read that was going through negative things in life and how they could use their imagination to get to the positive place. I know that imagination can be negative and is a process that would help.

After 2 years of searching for someone to help me with the publishing and someone that would not take my idea and use it for themselves, I found some help. Life can be very scary. People are not who they say they are. I, being a trusting person, found out that not everyone is always trusting. I also found out that they have other motives. I guess you can call this, backroom agendas. I have to be lead by the spirit of God. The Holy Spirit does not lie.

My first book was published and now I am on the second book. These stories are God given and I can only give God the credit for this.

When I Stepped Over The Rainbow

In order to step over the rainbow, these are the steps

1) What is your Purpose?

2) How will God get the Glory?

3) Teach others how you got there.

4) Continue to strive to make yourself better.

5) Death is not the end.

As I look at myself, I had to confront many issues. I was unsure of myself and always wanted to be in the background. I do not like people to tell me what to do. I like to be in control. I have learned that as long as I monopolize people that God cannot get the full glory of my life.

I like to play it safe. People are not what they say they are. I always take people for face value. I watch what you say and I watch what you do. I pray and ask God what is the purpose for you in my life. I have come to realize things just do not happen by chance.

People come and go. I have friends, but they are few. I am on my second marriage. I had to analyze why I married the first time and why the second time. These are subjects you will have to research to get to know why you do the things you do. I have had some painful things that have happened to me, in my life, but I do not like to air my dirty laundry, but we all have some. Right?

1) What is my purpose?

What is my purpose? This question I ask myself every day. It changes according to the things I am doing. This may be the same for you. First, I am someone's daughter. My purpose is to be a good child growing up and to learn the things that my parents have taught me. It is also my purpose to learn from the other people that God puts in my environment.

As a child, you have to learn the difference between good and bad things, for you. Some of this will come from the things you learn from your parents and others will come with trial and error.

I was always a loving child and I learned to love everyone. The first time I remember having some problems with people, was during school. This girl in my class always wanted to fight. I was not a fighter.

However, I can clearly remember my dad telling me, "If you come home crying about someone fighting you, I will give you a beating." I was able to weigh the odds and the next time she wanted to fight, those words came back to be. I was the victor. I never had any problems out of her concerning fighting.

As we develop through life, God puts you in places and around people that are able to teach you the things you will need to know to fulfill your purpose. Many times, we just do not listen, which is why we get side tracked or miss the track completely.

Once I had children, my purpose was to raise them to fulfill their purpose. I did not forget my main reason for being, but I did encourage my children to come along for the journey. I did not become their friend, because I was their parent. I made sure they had plans and goals. I showed them how I reached my goals. After awhile, this becomes contagious. People like to be around others that are successful. They want to know how you get there and how did you stay there.

It is very easy to get a Mercedes Benz but when it breaks down; did you ask God to make sure you have the money for repairs, tires, and the oil change? We forget to ask for all the needs.

I remember I had lost my job, my house was in foreclosure and I was raising two children by myself. I cried that night, thinking to myself "what am I going to do?" God told me to do something strange. I guess to test my faith. Every day, I would place pennies in the driveway. After awhile the entire driveway was full of pennies. God spoke to me and said, "Do you see all those pennies in the driveway, just like all the stars in the sky. You are my child and I will not let anything be taken from you."

The next day, I was blessed with a better job. The mortgage company worked out a plan for me to keep my house. I still have that house and I rent it out to a family that needed a beautiful place to live. God is true and He is just.

During those times when it seems like all hell has broken loose, that is when you have a party, just you and the Lord. The lack is in us. There is no lack in God. First, take some time and wherever you are in life ask God what is your purpose.

I am in my prime. My children are grown and now I have grandchildren. My purpose has changed many times during my life. I am writing now to let people know you can be whatever you want to be. Dream, Dream, Dream!

2) How can God get the Glory?

I was always a dreamer. I remember looking out my window and letting my mind just wonder. I thought everyone were dreamers. I was right. They are. Just like me, they were looking for love on the outside and were disillusioned. The children come and 20 years later, you are still trying to find out how to get from point A to point B.

God will get the glory when you tell people about Him. When you tell people that this BMW Z3 2010 is paid for, they look at you and think how? I do not sell drugs. I do not play sports.

I serve a God that told me some promises. Read the promise in the Bible. I was just so crazy that I took God at his word. He said he would give me the desires of my heart. Every time someone pulls up beside me. I say, to

God be the Glory!!!!!!. I am thankful for everything

Before I get out of bed, I say thank you Lord. When I get in bed at night, I say thank you. I remember my grandfather would say his prayers every morning and every night, even when he became sick. He lived with me at my home. He was barely able to walk and he would get on his knees. Sometimes, either my husband or I would have to help him get up.

There are some principles that you must make a daily part of your life in order to reach the goals that you have set. The first principle is to make sure that you pray about the things you want. Everything you want is not always what you need.

Second, when asking for these things you must believe you already have them. Then you must find the people that are where you want to be. The people that are living the life you want. This is a mind thing. If they can get it, then you can to. The next step, if it is easy then everyone would be doing these things, you must be willing to put all your energy into the tasks it takes to get the things you are striving for.

You must be willing to work day and night. Give up some things. While my friends were having parties and doing fun things I was working. However, once I had achieved the things I needed, I did not have to wait until the weekend to party or wait for birthdays or Christmas. I could have these special days every day.

You must stay focused. You must be able to listen to the still quiet voice within you. That is God speaking to you. If you listen to Him, He will not lead you astray and He will send the right people into your environment to lead you to the next step.

There is a trial and error lesson. You must learn from your mistakes (Life Lessons) or even better learn from the mistakes that others have done.

This can be painful and may be a setback. However, it is the person who takes these Life lessons and pushes forward to the goals ahead. I remember when I was going through a divorce it was painful and I saw how my children suffered from not having a father in the house. They speak about that now. But I had to weigh the odds to stay in a relationship that was going nowhere or to get out and free myself from the negative forces that only wanted to hold me back from my God given purpose.

I am glad I moved on. I have no hard feelings but I have learned to make myself happy and not allow people to give me the guidelines for what I feel happiness is for me. Reading has bridged the gap for all the things I wanted to accomplish. If I wanted to buy real estate, I would read books about this subject and follow the road map of the people who were successful.

You must set goals for your life and ask God to lead you to the places and people that will help you to accomplish these goals. I have learned that you cannot take these material things with you but that God does want you to occupy or be a good steward over the things he has given you. When acquiring these material objects they must not be just for you, but to help others. What is your motive? If I have 10 houses, I can only live in one at a time. If I have 4 cars, I can only drive one at a time. So what is the motive? I do not have to prove anything to people but that God can do and He will provide.

3) Teach others how you got there

Teaching others is easy if they are willing to learn. My problem is being able to discern who really wants to learn. Some people say they want to learn but they are not willing to be taught and they may not be willing to get up at 3:00 in the morning to write or travel to a place they have never been. I had to take chances and many people do not want to leave their comfort zone. I do understand this because you are going to a new place with new people and you do not know what the outcome will be. However, you have an idea that all will be well sometimes this will happen and sometimes, it may not. However, in going, you will learn something new. You will learn more about your strengths and weaknesses. You will meet new people and you will get new ideas. The mind is like a computer it inputs information. The more information you have the more options you will have when you are making decisions.

If you continue to do the same things, you will get the same results and most of the time these are the results that we do not want. So take a chance, break out of the box and try new things, let your mind get a chance to experience new people, places and things.

All people are teachable. People learn different ways. I learn from watching and from doing. Some people can learn from just listen to people. However, you learn is not important but that you learn. The way you know that you have learned something new, is that you are prospective of your old environment changes. If you learn a new word and the understanding of this word, it will give you a better understanding of other words. As time moves on you will begin to talk to people who use those words and then you will change your environment and then your train of thought begins to change. So, by learning something as small as a new word; it will change your entire life.

Time... This ticking clock has mastered the art of not staying still. We sometimes wonder; where did the time go? We also wonder what we did with that time. All this tells about the person and how they value themselves and the other people that are around them. I find people that value their time, also value the time of others. Then there are people who are time wasters they think that time will never run out. This fact is not true. Time never runs out, but life does. You never know when life will come to an end and so this makes time very important. Time is ever ticking and we must take the time to do the things that will be productive for ourselves and for those around us.

First when teaching people my first question is what do you want to learn? Many people do not know what they want. This is the first problem. When you do not know what you want, you will never focus on the subjects to get there. We all want to be happy, but what does happy mean to you? Happy to me was being healthy, wealthy, and serving God. These are my goals. I began by making sure I did not eat the wrong foods. I do like good food. To be wealthy I made a plan to acquire wealth (study how other wealthy people became wealthy) Serving God. (Read my bible daily and follow the guidelines).

Now, do not get me wrong, I did have some trials along the way. I did eat that fried pork chop some times and I did not always spend my money wisely and sometimes I did not do the things that God asked me to do. But during these times when I was not on the right path, I had some prices to pay. Never think that because you are doing what you feel is right that it is right. Sometimes and most of the times we do what we think is right at that time. However, even a few days later a better choice comes along. I have learned never to make a choice when under stress or pressure. I will always wait, sometimes until the next day to make a choice and I have learned to pray before I make a choice. God knows the best choice because he knows me and he knows that outcome of the situation and the

Robin Dozier- Ghent

Spirit never lies.

So you can learn from others and you will. God will teach you the people, places and things you need to learn from. I have found that if you go to that still quiet place you will never go too far off the path of your goals and desires.

Teaching about things you know, is good. However, most people watch how you do the things you do and if they see what they like, they will want to be like you. Jesus is a good example I want to be like him.

I can tell you how I became the person I am today and how I made it from A – B. When it all comes down to the bottom line, whom did you help? How did you treat the people that God allowed to come your way? Do you have an inner peace about yourself? The flesh is never satisfied. You always want more. If you eat today, you will be hungry in 15 minutes, so that is life. However, there is a deeper you, and this must be explored. The only way to find this part of you is to spend time with you. I have two children and I love them both the same. My oldest son does not like to be alone and because of this, he finds himself in destructive relationships. When you are anxious, you will grab the first think coming your way. Many time's it is not the right things. I have been the same way. If just made me more anxious about getting out of the mess I have gotten myself in to.

Time is there. We never know when it will stop for us

but we do know that it will. So take the time that you have and learn the things that will be a positive asset to you and the people around you.

4) Continue to strive to make yourself better

In trying to make yourself better, you have to look back at the things you have done and what was the outcome. My first marriage I was young and really did not know what love was and at that time, I was unhappy with myself. I had just finished college and was looking for a way to leave my mother's house. I met a man that had a lot of baggage but thought it would work because we loved each other. He was older than I was and had three other children and a failed marriage. I learned quite a lot in this marriage and I would not trade the life lessons for anything. Then the children started coming, my oldest son Christopher was the apple of my eye. We did everything together. I would even take him to class with me while I was finishing my college degree. We still have a strong bond and unconditional love for each other. Then the second child came, Jamele, he was a quiet child, not outgoing like Christopher. I remember he became very sick and when I took him to the Doctors, they said he had Rickets. This is a disease when you do not have enough Vitamin D and your bones do not develop right. His bones where soft and when he would try to walk it made his legs bow. At night, he would have to wear special shoes and there was a brace between the shoes like a bar. I can laugh at it now because he would try to get up at night to go to the bathroom and would not be able to walk and I could hear him fall out of his bunk bed. He slept on the bottom of the bed. He had to go to the doctors every 6 weeks to get Vitamin D shots. He is doing fine, now. Then, it was quite frightening. Any time your child is ill a mother worries about how will this child develop and how will he or she be able to make it in life. Everything turned out well, and he is a grown man and going to college and that is good.

I always enjoyed learning and I would expose my children to the finer things in life. I was raised to not be lazy. We were not allowed to watch a lot of television growing up. We had one TV in the living room and my mother would monitor what we watched. 60 minutes was one of the shows we could watch. On Saturday, my sister and I had to clean the house and our treat for this was to be able to stay up late and watch Saturday Night Live. We always went to church on Sunday. Sometimes the church would have special events for the teenagers. We would attend those events. Most of the time my mother would take us to the library and we would get books to read during the week. Once we became older, we would participate in Girls Scouts and then my mother would have us participate in the Fine Arts. We had swimming lessons, ballet and we also had to play an instrument. I chose the flute and my sister started out with the violin but changed to the trumpet. Every Saturday morning we would drive into Boston with our bag lunch and go to our lessons.

I always like to go to school. I have taken classes at the Museum of Fine Arts in Boston, Massachusetts and also at the Boston Conservatory. I liked speaking French I would have a tutor teaching me French, Father Fornier lived at a Catholic Monastery. I would go there to get French lessons. Summer time when most children are hanging out at the house as a break from the school year, I was off at camp. This started from the age of 9 years old until I was 16. I have been to Horseback riding camp, Mountain climbing camp, gymnastic camp even the Girl Scouts had a camp. I have been able to take care of myself for a while. That is why I am able to function in all types of situations now. I taught my children that you never judge a person. Take people for face value. What I mean is that you should never try to change a person to whom you think they should be. You have to reach them where they are now and as you become better friends, you can show them how you live your life and show them that you can be whatever you choose to be. Sometimes, this is hard because God sends all types of people into your life and you have to be able to know if that person is going to be an asset to you and a debt to you and your purpose.

I had to learn this by trial and error. I am a people person and I like being around people who want to make their lives better. Some people say they want to change, but they keep doing the same things, over, and over again. It is a hard thing to think that if you keep doing the same thing you will get a different result. You must pray for people that are trying to do better for themselves and not just talking but making changes in their lives to get the situations right .

Each day I made it a point to spend some time by myself and with the Lord. I found out that if you spend some time with Him in the morning before you leave your house and ask Him to direct your way He will. I also ask God to help me to be of service to someone in need that day. It could be as simple as "Hello" to someone who is having a bad day. Even while driving, and just letting a car in front of me. What is the rush in life? I heard a minister on the radio say Jesus walked everywhere he went and he was able to accomplish everything he needed to do in 33 years. I think that people rush because they have not planned the things they needed to do and when they take inventory, they feel they have lost time. Time can never be recovered. You have to start where you are and complete the task at hand then go on to the next task and before you know it, you have completed all that needs to be done.

Always try to better yourself. Reading bridged the gap for me. When I read about places I would like to visit, I can see the pictures in my mind. The imagination is a great way to stretch your thinking and be able to use your vivid imagination.

I always daydreamed, that is what they called it. Now, I am a visionary and I am able to visualize the plays I would like to go to and the inventions that will make this world a better place.

It took me a while to get to this point in life. When I turned 50, it was great. I am half of 100 and now I can do some of the things that I was afraid to do when I was 20 or even 30. My theory is if I do not do it now then when.

5) Death is not the End

I have worked in the funeral business for over 20 years. I have seen some great people leave this earth and I have seen some young people leave to soon. However, death is not the end. You are here for a reason. You are not a mistake. When you look at the odds for you not being born; they are great. There are a million sperms and only one egg. They are all fighting to get that one egg and one gets there, WOW. The bible says I knew you before you were conceived, before you were in your mother's womb. That means that God had a purpose for you before your mother and father had one. So while they try to teach you the things they know and do the best they can at that time. God form which we came and to which we will return knows you better.

Death is another state of living. You have a physical

body, and it becomes old and sometimes it becomes ill. At that point, you must leave that body here on the earth and it going back into the ground. We came from the dirt of the ground, and that is where it returns. The Spirit is the most important part. That is the Godly part of you. Even when you die, the Spirit will leave a legacy. When you do go, for others, they do not forget those things even when you are physically gone. When you do negative things, that to will be remembered. It is always good to try and leave a positive image of yourself with people. Sometimes it is hard to always be friendly because you are in the flesh but be able to forgive and leave a good impression of yourself to people. The world is a place where there should be love and peace but this is not always the way it ends up

It is hard to be happy all the time, because there are times when you will be sad. It is very important to look at the situation and make the best of it. When you have a loved one that dies, you are very sad and this is not a good time to be happy. You truly miss that person and sometimes you may question why they had to leave you? However, even in these times that is always a bright side because you can remember the good times you had with that person. This should bring a smile to your face and even warm your heart with joy for a brief moment.

I know a hard pill to swallow, is the death of a child. A mother will start to question herself, and ask what she's done to get such bad news. I should have gone before my child but we must take into consideration we are here for a short time and no one knows when or where.

It does not matter the age, race, or gender, death has no mercy. We must be able to take this lesson and use this time to cherish our loved ones and let the small issues go. Love is the key to every problem. Pure love will make a person be who they are.

It is always a pleasure to write and help other people and touch them with a kind word and a smile. Remember that this is a one-way journey and you must make the most of every day, and life is always pure Love.

www.ingramcontent.com/pod-product-compliance
Lightning Source LLC
Chambersburg PA
CBHW060104050426
42448CB00011B/2621